AF413350

Sam Houston State University:
It's Not Just a College, It's a Legacy

by Tiffani Jaqua

Illustrated by
Cristobal Carselle

Jaqua Publishing

DEDICATION

To my boys, Darren and Bryson, I hope you always continue to learn and enrich your educations.

Acknowledgements

I would like to give special thanks to Cristobal Carselle. Cris, you continue to amaze me with your creativity, adaptability and easygoing nature when working together. Nineteen books together so far…and counting. To Russell Martinez, AVP for Marketing and Branding at SHSU and Zack Jones, Director of Creative Design and Production at SHSU, thank you for your assistance in obtaining approval for publication. To Derrick Birdsall, Director of Sam Houston Memorial Museum, Charles Vienne, Executive Director of SHSU Alumni Association, and Breanna Dotson, Director of Campus Activities and Traditions, thank you for providing critical information about the traditions and history at Sam Houston State University. To Natalie Ghatalia and Alex Carrillo, thank you for gracing the back cover!

Attending Sam Houston State University,

Will have you feeling larger-than-life,

You see, Bearkats aren't just Bearkats for four years,

Bearkats are Bearkats for life!

79

In 1879, the college was founded as Sam Houston Normal Institute,

Opening in Huntsville, TX, with one building, 110 students and 4 member faculty,

It was the first tax-supported teacher training institution in Texas,

But, its name changed in 1923.

Sam Houston
Normal Institute
Est.1879

You see, in 1923, it initially changed to Sam Houston State Teachers College,

Yet, in 1965, it changed again to Sam Houston State College,

Only to change once again, in 1969, to its current name, Sam Houston State University,

Which the Texas Legislature agreed to acknowledge.

Sam Houston
State University
Est.187

It's named after Sam Houston, a

former U.S. Senator,

Who served in the U.S. Congress

for more than ten years,

He also led the Texan Army to

victory against Santa Anna,

During the Battle of San Jacinto,

it appears.

He's known for signing the Texas Declaration of Independence,

And he was a former governor of both Texas and Tennessee,

But leading Texas to its independence and defeating the Mexican Army,

Certainly secured his place in history.

His iconic statue is located on

Interstate 45 near campus,

Standing sixty-seven feet tall,

It's positioned on a ten foot

granite base,

And its grandeur is sure to

enthrall.

Sam Houston State University
has been designated as a high
research activity college,

By the Carnegie Classification of
Institutions of Higher Education,

And it's federally designated as a
Hispanic-Serving Institution and
Doctoral University,

Which is cause for celebration.

The first African-American

student, John Patrick,

Was admitted to SHSU in 1964,

Because integration changed

things and set a precedent,

So discrimination wouldn't happen

like before.

The school's fight song debuted in 1947,

With lyrics written by Patti Morton and Florence Hughes,

It's based on the melody of Semper Paratus,

Which is the same one the U.S. Coast Guard band members use.

SHSU's motto, "The measure of a Life is its Service",

Was created by Harry Estill,

It was first inscribed on Old Main's window,

And found on the western wall of Frank Parker Plaza (formerly Bearkat Plaza), still.

"THE MEASURE OF A LIFE IS ITS SERVICE"
Sam Houston State University Motto

Also along the western edge of
Frank Parker Plaza,

You'll find the Blatchley Bell
Tower,

It stands fifty-feet tall as an
iconic landmark on campus,

And can be heard playing music
upon every hour.

First used as an original building

of Austin College from 1850-76,

You'll find the most interesting

and oldest building of all,

It was also used by Mitchell

College from 1877-79,

And is known as Austin Hall.

The Newton Gresham Library is actually the third library to open on the campus,

Following behind the Peabody (1901-1928) and Estill (1928-1968),

Although the previous two locations are no longer serving as libraries,

Both buildings have been uniquely repurposed and serve the university, still.

But the popular Newton Gresham
Library, or NGL, opened in 1968,

Comprising four floors, each an
acre in size and filled with rows
and rows of bookcases,

Its vast literary content offers
students and staff tremendous
research opportunities,

And provides students the
opportunity to reserve quiet
study spaces.

7R

The Lowman Student Center, also known as the LSC,

Includes quite a few options for student dining,

It's also where friends often meet up for study groups,

To ensure their college grades won't start declining.

Sam-Fil-A
SAMW

It's located in the heart of campus,

And home to Paw Print Food Court and University Campus Bookstore,

There you'll also find a theater, a bowling alley and a ballroom,

And many, many other places to explore.

10% OFF!
SH

Although the first athletic teams at SHSU were known as the "Normals",

The slogan "Eat 'em up Kats" now embraces the wonderful Bearkat spirit,

It's used to depict a fighting stance against Bearkat rivals,

So fairly often you will hear it.

EAT 'EM
UP KATS!

The Bearkat is the school's official mascot and originally named after the Kinkajou,

A carnivorous South American mammal which is known to be fiercely admired,

He's now fondly known as Sammy Bearkat, who once had a mascot partner, Samantha,

That all changed in 2005, when Samantha Bearkat was retired.

Since 1923, the orange and white Bearkat has been a recognizable symbol,

To Sam Houston State University and vital,

But Sammy Bearkat, the current mascot of the university,

Hasn't always held that prestigious title.

You see, an unofficial mascot was

a stray dog named Tripod,

Who roamed the campus from

approximately 1948-1962,

And even though it's rumored he

had a lame left-front paw,

Students and faculty adored him

through and through.

Former SHSU President Harmon Lowman gave a eulogy at Tripod's funeral,

And Tripod was buried on campus between Belvin-Buchanan Hall and Old Main Memorial,

Dan Rather, a former SHSU alumnus, American journalist and news anchor,

Even wrote about Tripod in a memorable editorial.

In Loving memory...

Homecoming is an eventful week of activities,

Including a parade down Sam Houston Avenue with tons of floats,

Be sure to look for the Bearkat Marching Band and Homecoming court royalty,

Because the king and queen will be announced on the field after the votes.

HOMECOMING
HOMECOMING

One of the university's best known past traditions was the "Battle of the Piney Woods",

An annual football game against S.F.A.,

You see, Stephen F. Austin was SHSU's biggest rivalry from 1923-2022,

When S.F.A's Lumberjacks first traveled to Huntsville to play.

The annual game was played at NRG Stadium in Houston,

And the annual pep-rally, Firefest, was held before each Battle of the Piney Woods game,

Where students rallied and made proclamations of winning,

And the bonfire was set aflame.

"The March 2 the Grave" is another unique SHSU tradition,

Celebrating General Sam Houston's life and Texas' Independence,

Students and faculty march from campus to Sam Houston's grave at Oakwood Cemetery,

Beginning in 1893, it continues to draw huge crowds in attendance.

The current Sam Houston State University ring was unveiled in 2003,

And now all SHSU rings are uniquely identifiable,

To order, students must have successfully completed seventy-five credits,

Or their applications will be unjustifiable.

Austin Hall is depicted on one side of the ring,

With Sam Houston represented on the opposing side,

The star on the crest of the ring represents the state of Texas,

And the word "honor" is engraved inside.

Juniors and seniors wear their rings with the school name facing them,

And during commencement, rings are turned outward for all to see,

This represents graduates are ready to share their knowledge with the world,

And that each graduate has completed that hard-earned degree.

Sam Houston State University

All SHSU rings are housed and guarded overnight in Sam Houston's historic home,

On the eve of each ring ceremony, as a unique school tradition,

It's located on the grounds of the Sam Houston Memorial Museum and Republic of Texas Presidential Library,

An honorary title addition.

Since first established in 1921,
"The Tree of Light",

Has been one of the university's
oldest traditions celebrated each
year,

And although it's a 42-foot
artificial tree in Frank Parker
Plaza that's now the gathering
spot,

"The Tree of Light" is an event
many continue to hold dear.

The original evergreen cedar

tree is located in the middle of

Evans Complex,

Marked with a plaque

documenting its history for all to

see,

It's become one of SHSU's most

iconic landmarks,

Especially since it's a monumental

and colossal tree.

Sam Houston State University,

Is a school steeped in culture, history and tradition,

And with its unique traditions and unparalleled accolades,

It's a phenomenal place to learn...for anyone with ambition.

BEARKA
SH

Find the definitions for any vocabulary words you don't know on this page. A few vocabulary words are listed below.

debut—

designated—

embraces—

engraved—

grandeur—

inscribed—

landmark—

precedent—

proclamations—

unveiled—

List any other new vocabulary words you discovered.

1.

2.

3.

4.

5.

6.

7.

8.

9.

10.

Imagine you're the illustrator and draw your own pictures of your favorite Sam Houston State University traditions or experiences.

List sets of rhyming words you found in this book.
Ex.) *tradition and ambition*

1.

2.

3.

4.

5.

6.

7.

8.

9.

10.

ABOUT THE AUTHOR

Tiffani Jaqua ("Jakeway") is a Texas A&M University graduate... class of '90 and Sam Houston State University master's degree graduate, class of '96. She has worked in education and counseling for nearly thirty years. She is widowed and lives with her two sons in The Woodlands, Texas. This is her nineteenth book. Inspiration for this book stems from fond memories as a master's degree student at Sam Houston State University.

ABOUT THE ILLUSTRATOR

Cristobal Carselle is a young artist, college student and aspiring illustrator based in Houston, Texas. He has been drawing and painting for over a decade. He has received many awards for his work. This is his eighteenth illustrated book with Tiffani Jaqua, and he plans on working on many more projects.

If you enjoyed this book, check out Tiffani Jaqua's other books, available at tiffanijaqua.com.

<u>Blowing Dandelions with Sea Lions</u> (2018) A collection of 54 rhyming poems and illustrations on various topics such as sunburns, sleepovers, dilemmas with braces, school topics, travel, swim team problems and other sports, rude hamsters, turtles and other pets

<u>It's My Turn in the Front Seat</u> (2020) A collection of 54 rhyming poems and illustrations on various topics such as insane bus drivers, cafeteria food and other school topics, birthdays, soccer mishaps and other sports, travel, squirrels, raccoons, swimming dogs and other pets

<u>The Students in Room 109</u> (2020) A collection of 54 rhyming poems and illustrations on various topics such as picky eaters, doctor visits, travels, ant farms, frog trouble and other pets, asking too many questions, treehouses, sports, picture day and other school topics

<u>Questions for Santa</u> (2021) A rhyming poetry/activity book about all things Santa Claus related

<u>Questions for the Easter Bunny</u> (2021) A rhyming poetry/activity book about all things Easter Bunny related

<u>Questions for the Tooth Fairy</u> (2021) A rhyming poetry/activity book about all things Tooth Fairy related

<u>Halloween Things</u> (2021) A rhyming poetry/activity book about Halloween related topics

<u>Traveling Around the World</u> (2021) A rhyming poetry/activity book about locations around the world and traveling

<u>Distinctively Diverse Dinosaurs</u> (2021) A rhyming poetry/activity book about dinosaur facts

<u>Phases of the Moon</u> (2021) A rhyming poetry/activity book about the eight phases of the lunar cycle

<u>Phenomenally Pragmatic Penguins</u> (2021) A rhyming poetry/activity book about penguin facts

<u>Questions for the Leprechaun</u> (2022) A rhyming poetry/activity book about all things St. Patrick's Day related

<u>Questions for a Princess</u> (2022) A rhyming poetry/activity book about all things related to fairytale princesses

<u>Questions for a Pirate</u> (2022) A rhyming poetry/activity book about pirate life

<u>Texas A&M University: It's Not Just a College, It's a Culture</u> (2022) A rhyming poetry/activity book about Aggieland traditions.

<u>Louisiana State University: It's Not Just a College, It's a Community</u> (2023) A rhyming poetry/activity book about Tigerland traditions.

<u>The University of Texas: It's Not Just a College, It's a Civilization</u> (2023) A rhyming poetry/activity book about Longhorn traditions

<u>The Problem with My Cat's Meow</u> (2024) A rhyming poetry/activity book about a cat's strange "meow" and mimicking other animals it encounters

<u>Splendidly Sensational Sea Turtles</u> (2024) A rhyming poetry/activity book about sea turtle facts, endangerment and conservation efforts